## Dedication

For the ones who still believe in love, even after heartbreak, who carry hope like a quiet prayer, even when it trembles in their hands...this book is for you. May you find yourself in these pages,
 and may you never stop believing that love, in all its forms, will always find its way back to you.

And in a time to come you will meet someone whose love is a rhythm worth dancing to.

Heavy on choosing peace, unapologetically.

Flowers, handwritten love notes, well-thought-out dates, mind stimulating conversation, eye gazing, forehead kissing kinda vibes.

Spa day, comedy show, candle making, wine tasting, candlelit rowboat dinner, cozy cabin weekend getaway type of energy.

Let's turn on a playlist and watch the sunset from a parked car while eating our favorite snacks and laughing the night away.

You may be compatible with them based upon who you are today, but do they have the capacity to evolve to accommodate the person you'll grow to become tomorrow? Compatibility and capacity are essential.

Sometimes God allows connections to sever that were never meant for us in the first place. We thought it was them, but it was really Him.

Send you flowers and a handwritten card on a random day once a week so that you're always surprised when they arrive, while simultaneously sending your mom a bouquet as a thank you for making you.

In the mood to love one person in every way for the rest of my life.

Let's meditate face-to-face in nature sitting Indian- style with interlocked hands while taking slow and deep breaths and staring into each other's eyes.

I hired a housekeeper to clean our place three times a week and private chef to prepare meals for us at our convenience because I understand how large of a responsibility it is to manage a home, nurture children, and make time for your individual passions while being attentive to me.

Every time I hear this song it reminds me of you... kinda vibes.

I love who you're becoming, but I adore who you are.

You are enough. Who you are today is enough.

Intentional about you.

I believe in you and I'm going to help you win.

I pray for you because I know God can heal parts of your heart that I would never be able to reach.

Let's go to therapy together not because there's anything wrong but because I want us to be intentional about growing closer.

Let's build a fort in the living room and watch our favorite 90's sitcoms while eating our favorite snacks in matching pajamas.

I don't want anyone else but you.

Let's fill a basket with a thermos of homemade soup, an extra large hoagie, our favorite chips , and a couple slices of cake and have an autumn picnic while watching colorful leaves fall and keeping each other warm from the brisk breeze.

Pack your bags because I booked us a trip to Santorini, Greece and we leave in three days..

I saw this while I was out and remember you mentioning that you wanted it so I brought it for you.

You are extremely valuable to me and my life is better with you in it.

I take pride in creating an environment that allows you to rest in your softness and femininity. You don't have to be strong around me.

Wherever you are is home to me because you are home.

I love teaching you what I know and I'm intentional about it because pouring into my life partner is one of the best investments I could ever make.

I know relationships aren't easy and can be a lot of work, but I'll put the work in for you, because you're worth it.

Put a call in to the owner of a fully committed restaurant to get us in, tell you to be ready at 7:30 pm on Friday night for me to pick you up for our date, greet you with a bouquet of roses and lilies when I arrive, and invest the night away overindulging in the flavor of a conversation that tastes even better than the food on our plates.

I'll get mean about you. I'll offend them to protect us.

If being vulnerable is weak for a man, I'm willing to be weak in order to have a fruitful relationship with you.

I'm grateful for your presence in my life, and I hope that nothing in this life ever causes us to let each other go.

You are beautiful on every level - spiritually, physically, mentally, and emotionally - and I will always choose to see the good in you.

I take accountability for anything that I have done to hurt you and I apologize, because I refuse to allow pride to contaminate our union.

I find joy in knowing you, loving you, and accepting you completely.

I want to share my life with you.

I apologize for every person that told you they loved you and didn't mean it. I apologize for every time you loved someone with childlike faith, trusting that things would be different and they ended up the same. I apologize for those that picked fruit from your garden, but lacked the capacity to cultivate it's soil. I apologize, and I ask you to forgive me...for them.

Let's pray together, read together, and grow spiritually together.

You are the manifestation of the person I've always dreamed of being with and I'll never let anything or anyone come between us.

You're the baddest and I love to show you off.

I'm so proud of how diligent you are about building your business and I want to invest. Let's talk about it in Bali.

Send you edible arrangements, a teddy bear lightly sprayed with my cologne, balloons, and a gift card to Starbucks in the middle of the day just because.

Let's get away to a cabin and spend our time laughing, reading, talking, and cuddling in matching pajamas as the embers of a lit fireplace dance in the background.

Let's sit face-to-face and eye gaze to the sound of our own exhales as the sun sets through floor to ceiling windows in our peripheral.

I love you beyond the feeling. I am committed even in moments when I may not feel it.

Let's watch the sun rise over the ocean's horizon from the balcony while eating fruit and sipping herbal tea.

Cuddle and pray for you while you sleep.

Date night in another city.

You are altogether beautiful, my darling, and there is no blemish in you. -King Solomon

It's an honor to show up for you in your darkest moments. I have capacity for your lows. Come and cry on me.

Thinking of all the ways I can win your heart all over again every single day.

You're everything I've ever wanted. There's nobody for me but you.

Intentional about exploring you beyond your attractive exterior, for it is those moments that I discover your beauty.

Intentional about loving you with my decisions. I will continually choose you.

Every day I fall more in love with your soul. I adore the deepest parts of you.

Ladies, send a man in your life (significant other, brother, father, son, uncle, friend) this text:

I want you to know that I see you. I see the sacrifices that you make to be the man that you are. I'm thankful for you.

You give me a feeling that I've never felt before and I adore it.

Take her car, detail it, gas it up, then sit money in her cup holder.

I'm a generous man. I find joy in giving to and providing for you.

Let's build trust, build a healthy relationship, build a healthy marriage, build a house from the ground up, then build a family.

And in those moments when the feeling of romance relinquishes its pinnacle may we laugh together as best friends and love each other like family.

Good food.
Long flights.
Deep feelings.

Let's wake up to breakfast in Bora Bora.

It's an honor for me to create an environment that you never have to be strong in. I only want you to be soft here.

Her: Don't worry about dinner. I'm cooking for you tonight.

Him: I'll bring a bottle of wine and dessert.

I am committed to us, and I don't want anyone else to have me but you.

Ladies, send a man in your life (significant other, brother, father, son, uncle, friend) this text:

I pray that the veil between your dreams and your reality would become nonexistent. I pray that you reach every goal. I'm rooting for you.

Morning walk with you sipping hot beverage of choice, brunch at 11:30 am, spa at 2 pm, shopping at 6 pm, followed by us in pajamas watching a rom-com by 9 pm.

POV: I arrive to pick you up for Sunday brunch. I get out, come around to the passenger side, give you a gentle hug, and open your passenger door. You're greeted with red roses on the center console.

You're expensive AND I gladly afford you.

Sunsets and forehead kisses.

I never hesitate to compliment you on things that have nothing to do with your physical appearance, because I see value in you beyond your beautiful exterior.

Undress her mind until her thoughts stand naked before you. True intimacy is transparency.

I love it when you stare into my eyes and tell me exactly what you want.

Not gonna lie...women that know how to cook and love to do it are in a league of their own.

Rainy weather. Homemade soup slowly simmering on the stove. A soft blanket draped around us. Taking a deep dive into each other's emotional history while playing a card game.

I'm gonna always stand on business about you.

I found a new restaurant that I want us to try together.

I will fight for you. I will fight pride. I will fight temptation. I will fight the version of myself that I was yesterday to be the person that I'm supposed to be today. I. Will. Fight. For. You.

I just want to remind you that God is with you.

You're on my mind in the most pleasant way possible, and your presence in my life is a gift.

Tell me about your day while I rub your feet.

If you're reading this right now this is proof that you're never too far for God to reach.

I don't ever want to do anything to you that I wouldn't want done to me. Mindful of you with my decisions.

Him: I don't want anyone but you.

Her: Show me.

You're not too much. You're just right.

My desire for you is not based upon need or dependence. I want you here. For I am in love with your soul.

Marry me.

You make forever feel like a moment.

When you've done the work on yourself you can't afford to waste that work on the wrong person.

Let's hop in the car and take a light night drive to get tacos while listening to our favorite 90's groups.

I get joy breathing the air around you, for you smell like heaven.

In every language...

I love you
Te quiero
Je t'aime
Ich liebe dich
Ik houd van jou
Seni seviyorum

Show you kindness and consideration that you don't have to request or demand.

I pray that we make it through 100% of our bad days together. I can weather any storm as long as you're with me.

Come eat this food I made for you.

The person that sent this to you wants you to know that you are an asset in their life and they are thankful for your presence in it.

Pray over you and your business and then invest in it.

Consistent with you.

You deserve abundant, gentle, intentional love.

Them: When are you going to be in a relationship?

Me: When I meet someone who inspires my heart to love them romantically AND I receive confirmation from God that "this is your one."

I get my heart from my mother. She is the most loving, affirming, sweet, gentle, kind-hearted, and affectionate woman I know. I feel so fortunate to have been birthed and nurtured by her.

I don't know who said chivalry is dead but it's alive over here.

Let me know when you make it home safely.

I don't want to spend another Valentines Day without you.

Exotic fragrances and pheromones...

Have you eaten?

Pretty for no reason.

If you are experiencing deep sadness, loneliness, and/or struggle with comparison because of singleness this is a gentle reminder that your value is not based upon being chosen. You are loved, you are beautiful, and you are valuable.

Two things we're gonna always do is eat and laugh...

We see each other alot but I want to see you more...

Show me where your heart hurts. Let me kiss it.

You deserve the best so I gave you me.

My biggest flex is that your heart is safe with me.

I'm focused on you if you're focused on me.

Fumbling you is like winning the lottery and going broke again.

Good for your nervous system.

I just want to protect you.

There's a difference between attraction and intention.

I can look at you and tell that God paused everything to focus on making you.

I've seen a lot of things but you gave my heart eyes to see you.

Provide for you.
Protect you.
Prioritize you.

You feel like home to me and I'm ready to come inside.

Let's pray together.

And in the blink of an eye I was in love with you...

I don't play about you.

And suddenly, you became my truth.

I love you unconditionally. Forever.

Captivated by your mind, fascinated by your thoughts, enamored with...you.

There's beauty in two imperfect people showing up with the desire to be better every day.

Know your value and let it price them out.

Committed spouse, beautiful house, good food, great sex, and some well- behaved children.

That "forever love" is closer than you think.

## About The Author

Nathanael Cottman is a writer with a gift for turning raw emotion into beautifully curated truths. Through his deeply personal and reflective voice, he explores love, loss, healing, and the quiet moments in between. His work speaks to those who have felt unseen, offering solace in shared experiences and the beauty of vulnerability.

Flowers From Forgotten Fields is a testament to Nathanael's belief that even the emotions we try to bury have a way of blooming again —reminding us of who we are and where we've been. Through his writing, he invites readers to embrace their own stories with honesty and tenderness.

Connect with him on all platforms:
@fromnatewithlove

Made in the USA
Columbia, SC
16 March 2025